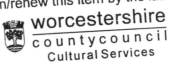

Where to find things

My Art Class

Here is a collection of creative crafts to make with children in your very own art class at home.

It's time to get your friends together and have an arty time! The best thing is you don't have to spend lots of money to be creative. All the ideas in this book are inspired by materials found in our own kitchens, such as cups, beans, and paper plates. One confession: I did go down to the local store for just a few bits and bobs! Have fun and go for it!

Nellie Shepherd

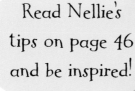

Read Nellie's tips on page 46 and be inspired!

Basic Kit

As well as the equipment pictured with each project, you will need the following basic kit:

card

paper

paint

felt-tip pens

PVA glue

scissors

stapler

tape (masking tape is best)

pots (for paint and glue)

paintbrushes

pipe cleaners

play dough

straws

fabric

Keep your art kit in a box so you can find it easily!

Helping hand

All the projects in this book are designed for young children to make, but they should only be attempted under adult supervision. Extra care should be taken when using sharp equipment, such as scissors, staplers, and pipe cleaners, and with small objects that may cause choking. Only use PVA or other non-toxic, water-soluble glue.

Ship Shape

flat
scourer

straw

glitter glue

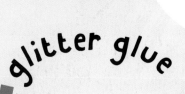

Cut a shape
From kitchen sponge
To make a little boat.
Put it in the water
And see if it will float.

sponge
scourer

You can use...

sponge scourers

glitter glue

flat scourers

straws

How to make it!

cut

Cut two corners off a sponge scourer to make a boat shape. You can glue the cut-off corners onto your boat to make a cabin.

cut again

Cut a flat scourer to make a sail. What shape sail are you choosing? Use glitter glue to decorate – it's such fun!

thread

Cut two slits – one at the top and one at the bottom of your sail. Thread a straw through the slits to make a mast.

push

Make a slit right in the centre of your boat (but not through the bottom). Push the mast into the hole. Use glitter glue to secure it.

Ahoy there!

finish

Finish decorating your boat. Then put it on water and have a splash!

8

Kid's talk
"I want to make another one for my daddy to play with."
Tom, age 2 ¾

Posh Pegs

peg

glitter

These sparkly pegs
Are the new kind of jewel.
Wear them anywhere.
They look really cool!

You can use...

glue

wooden pegs

card

ribbon

glitter

Tot Tip!

Posh pegs make a perfect necklace when you clip them on ribbon. Or try clipping them on an ordinary necklace so it looks extra special!

Here we go!

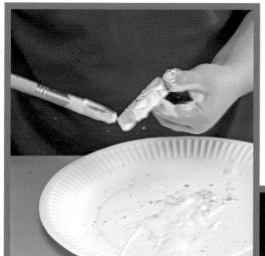

brush

Posh party to go to? Forget diamonds!
Instead make a set of posh pegs! First,
brush your pegs all over with glue.

roll

Roll your sticky pegs in
glitter. Use extra glue and
glitter if your pegs are not
completely covered.

clip

Let your pegs dry, then clip them onto ribbon.
Wear them around your neck, waist, or wrist.

peg

Get really carried away and clip the
pegs onto a strip of card to make
a posh-peg crown. It's the tops!

Did you know? The Queen of England's poshest jewels are called the crown jewels.

Dolly Mixers

Here are two wooden dolls.
Don't they look jolly?
One is called Bill
And the other is called Polly.

wooden spoon

I'm Polly!

I'm Bill!

pipe cleaner

pasta

paper napkin

You can use...

cardboard box

wool

glue

felt-tip pens

pasta

dried beans

card

wooden spoons

tissue paper

rice

napkin

pipe cleaners

felt

paint

Tot Tip!

Decorating and dressing your doll is brilliant fun – and it's much easier when you lay the spoon flat on the table.

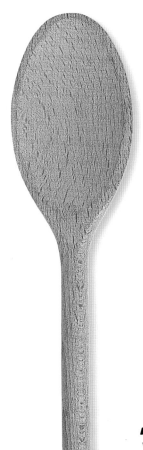

15

How to make it!

paint

Choose a doll to make, or design your own. Now paint the wooden spoon and stick on wool or rice for hair. Use felt, dried beans, or a felt-tip pen to make a face.

dress

There are lots of ways to dress your doll. You can cut an outfit from card and decorate it with felt-tip pens. Or cut out felt clothes and stick them straight onto your doll.

more ways to dress

We dressed Polly in a napkin skirt. Pipe cleaners, tissue paper, and pasta made great belts. We used dried beans for buttons and felt for hands and feet.

make a hat

Our Polly has a little hat made from a cardboard box. You can also make hats from paper cake cases, coffee filters, or whatever else you fancy!

balloon

wool

plastic cup

We're going up!

Cup, Cup, and Away!

Take a plastic cup
And tie on a balloon.
Give your little toys a ride
Some sunny afternoon.

18

You can use...

plastic cup

wool

glue

glittery stars

balloons

tissue paper

Tot Tip! This makes a mega mess! Don't forget to put down lots of newspaper.

You can do it!

blow up

Have fun blowing up your balloon! Tie on a length of wool. Then hang up the balloon so you can reach all around it (we hung ours from a washing line).

stick

Add a little water to your glue. Tear or cut shapes from tissue paper and stick them all over your balloon. Use at least three layers of tissue. You can add glittery stars (made from paper and glitter) if you like.

wrap

To make the basket, wrap wool around the plastic cup. Attach the basket to your balloon by taping more lengths of wool under the basket and to the balloon. Then find one or two little passengers to enjoy the ride!

Kid's talk
"I don't want it
to blow away so
I hold it with
my finger."
Ciciley, age 3

King of the Kitchen

You're the king of the kitchen
In your apron and your crown.
You're the best-dressed cook
This side of town!

glitter crown

peg

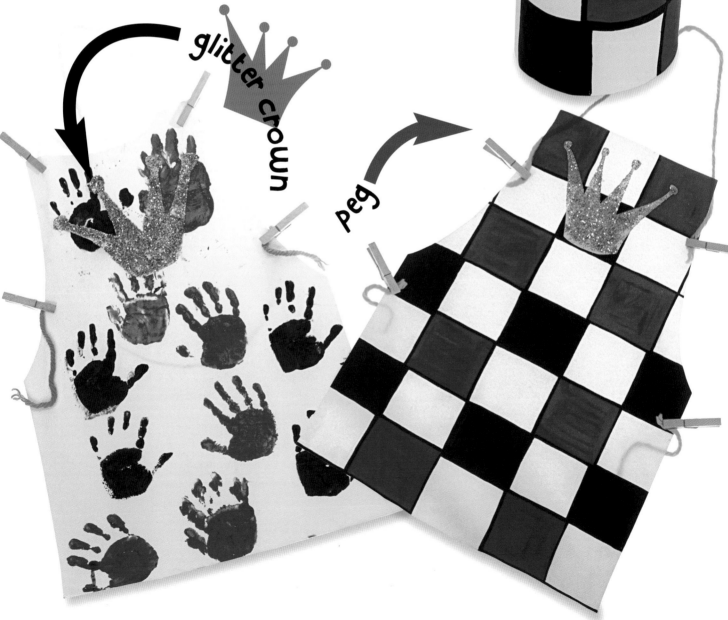

You can use...

glue

wool

glitter

Paint

sponge scourer

pegs

kitchen utensils

card

Here we go!

cut

Cut an apron shape from card. Dip little hands in paint and make handprints, or use a sponge or paintbrush to decorate the apron – it's up to you!

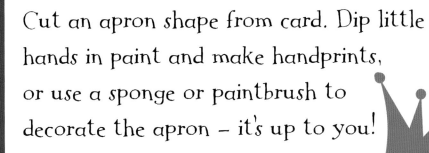

peg

Peg lengths of wool to the sides of your apron so you can tie it at the back. Add a loop at the top for your head.

Thread kitchen utensils onto another length of wool for decoration – and fun!

cut out a crown

Cut out a crown from card and decorate it to match your apron. Use pegs to hold the crown together. For a finishing touch, make a little glitter crown from more card and stick it on your apron.

24

Chickpea Shaker

tissue paper

card

glitter

Shake, rattle, and roll!

I'm a little chickpea shaker,
And I make a rattling noise.
You can shake me up and down,
And keep me with your toys.

You can use...

plastic cups

card

glitter

tissue paper

glue

dried chickpeas

How to make it!

tape

This project is so easy peasy! To make a good musical shaker, half fill a plastic cup with dried chickpeas. Tape it to another plastic cup.

stick

Wrap a half-oval shape of card around the plastic cups. Staple the pointed ends in place to make a tail. Stick tissue paper all over.

finish

To finish our chick, we glued on tissue-paper eyes, plus a card beak, wings, and feet. Then we covered her in glitter.

Tot Tip!

Make a chickpea shaker and shake along to Old MacDonald Had a Farm!

29

Flowers Fantastic

knives
and
forks

spoons

tissue
paper

These flowers
are as fantastic
As any flowers can be.
But what are they
made from?
Plastic cutlery!

paper plate

You can use...

paint

plastic cutlery

sand

glitter

tissue paper

You can do it!

tape

Tape together the plastic cutlery so it looks a bit like a bunch of flowers. Stand the flowers in a cup or bowl (you can push them into play dough to stop them falling over).

paint

Mix paint with a splodge of glue and a little sand. Paint the mixture all over your plastic flowers.

scrunch

Scrunch up little pieces of tissue paper, felt, or whatever else you fancy, and stick them onto the painted flowers to look like petals.

roll

Roll a paper plate into a cone to make a vase. Tape it in place and decorate it with paint, glitter, or anything pretty. Fill the vase with your flowers.

Sweet Belinda

I'm a sweetie!

paper plate

plastic spoon

glacé cherry

Kitchen foil

My name is Belinda
And I'm really very sweet.
I'm made from yummy things,
But I'm not for you to eat.

You can use...

food colouring

honey

icing sugar

plastic spoons

paper plates

rice paper

paper fastener

glacé cherries

Use hundreds and thousands, kitchen foil, or anything you like to make Belinda look lovely. Then let her set in the fridge.

Tot Tip!

How to make it!

mix

Make your own paint by mixing icing sugar with water and a little food colouring. Make different colours for Belinda's head, body, and hair.

brush

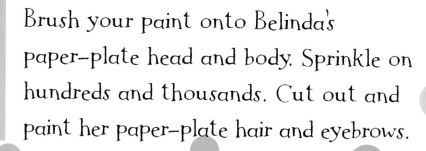

Brush your paint onto Belinda's paper-plate head and body. Sprinkle on hundreds and thousands. Cut out and paint her paper-plate hair and eyebrows.

stick

Using honey as glue, stick on glacé cherries for Belinda's buttons and nose. Stick on and paint her rice-paper eyes. Staple on Belinda's hair and eyebrows.

tape

We used a paper fastener to attach Belinda's head to her body, but you can just as easily use tape. Tape on plastic spoons for arms and legs.

dress up

To dress up Belinda, give her kitchen-foil bows and a cherry handbag made from a whole glacé cherry with a pipe cleaner pushed into either side.

Did you know?
Bees make honey to feed themselves during the winter. As they make more honey than they need, people eat the excess – and artists use it as glue!

Sea-through Sub

straw periscope

whoosh whoosh

wool

plastic bottle

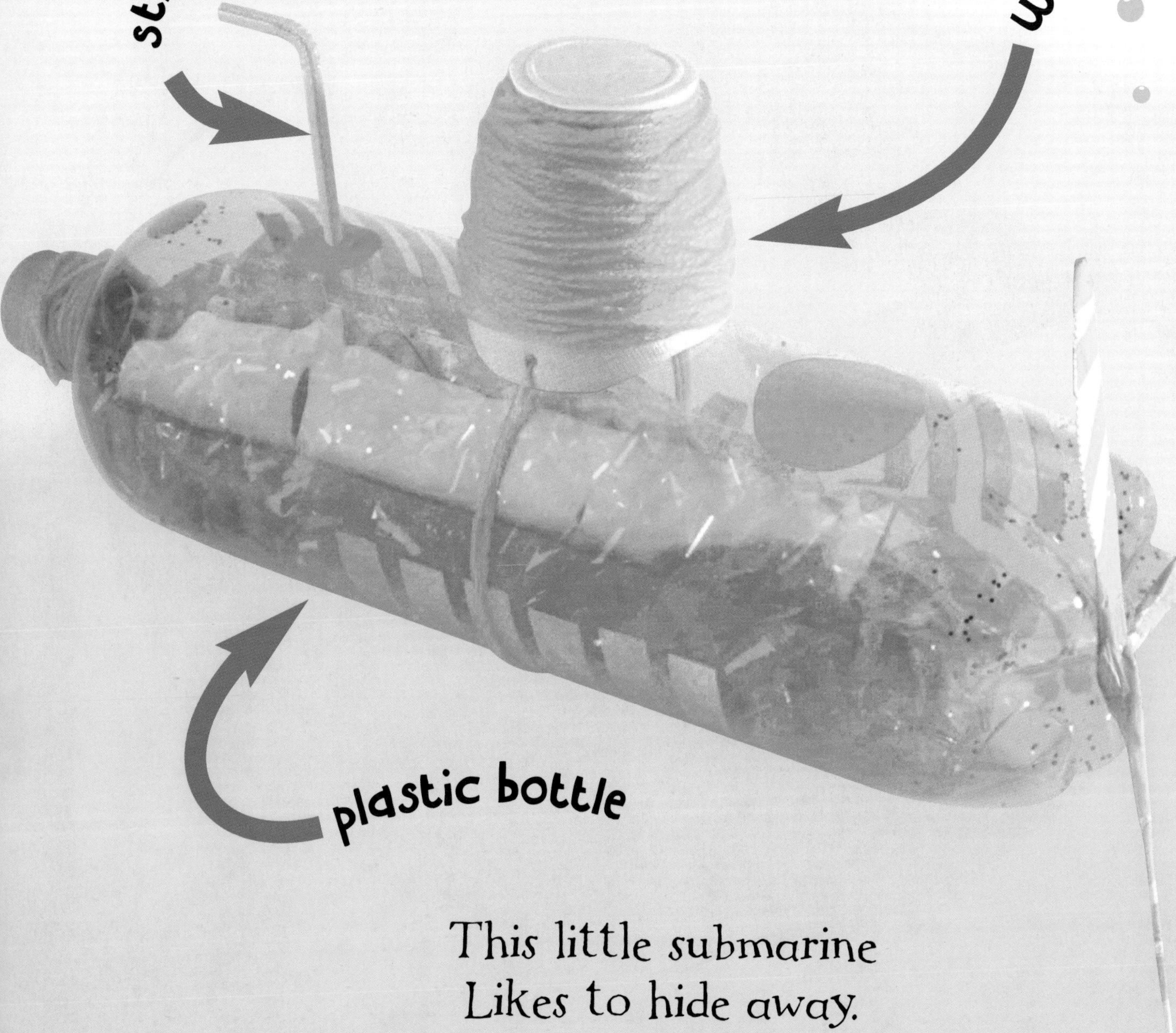

This little submarine
Likes to hide away.
It dives under the water
And sneaks about all day!

coloured tape

cellophane

wool

plastic knives

plastic cup

plastic bottle

glitter

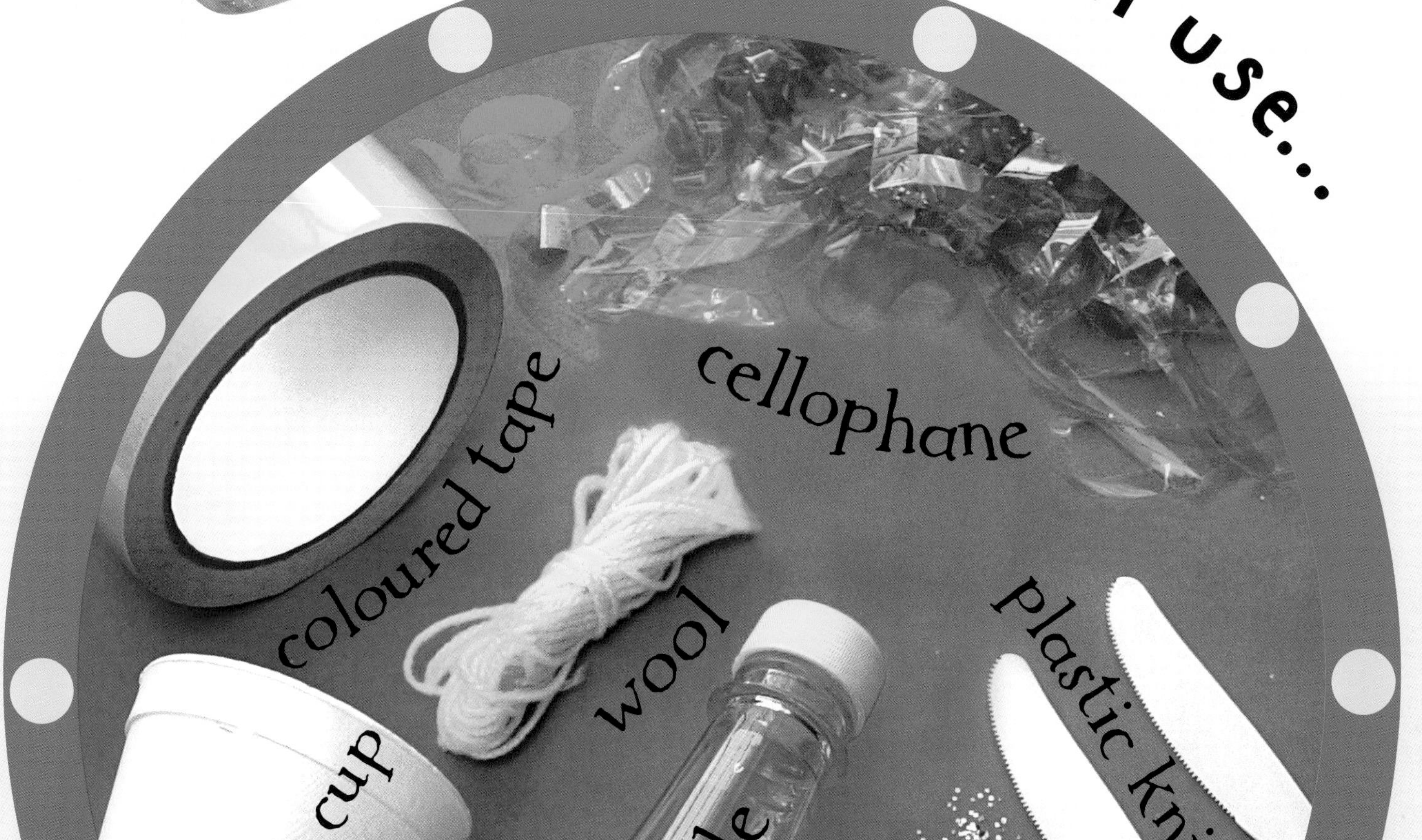

gurgle gurgle

Here We go!

soak

First soak the label off an empty plastic bottle. Make sure the bottle is completely dry. Then decorate the outside with coloured tape.

stuff

Stuff coloured cellophane into the bottle. Then pour in glitter. This is such fun to do! The glitter sticks to the insides of the bottle with no help at all!

tie

To make the turret, wrap wool around a plastic cup, then tie the cup to your bottle.

tape

Make a propeller by taping together two plastic knives. Stick them onto the bottle. For a periscope, tape on a straw.

dive!

We poured water into our submarine to help it dive under water.

Did you know?
People work, eat, and sleep in real submarines. They live in them for months at a time!

sweetie wrapper

Make a wish
at the wishing tree,
And perhaps
it will come true.
Then ask your friends
to come along
And make
their wishes, too.

kitchen foil

twig

sugar

sweetie

Wishing Tree

You can use...

play dough

plastic cup

Paint

sugar

twigs

paper plate

sweeties

kitchen foil

sweetie wrappers

You can do it!

push in

This is such a sweet idea! To make the wishing tree, put a lump of play dough into a plastic cup and push in twigs.

paint

Mix paint with a little glue. Paint the twigs all over, then leave them to dry.

tie

Now make your tree look lovely! Tie sweetie wrappers to the twigs using strips of kitchen foil.

cover

Cover a plate with kitchen foil and put your tree on it. Sprinkle sugar in the cup and all over the plate. Decorate the plate with sweeties, then you can make a wish!

Kid's talk
"This tree grows sweets. They're not ready yet."
Tom, age 2 ¾

Nellie's Knowledge

I've been teaching my art class to children for over ten years. Along the way, I've discovered a few tips that make the classes brilliant fun – and help bring out the creativity in all of us!

Organisation
It's good to have all the things you need before you start. But if you haven't got something, just improvise and use something else!

Inspiration
Look at all sorts of bits and bobs. What can you make them into? Challenge yourself and be inspired!

Fun factor!
Think about inviting friends over to join in. Play music and have a story break. It makes such a difference.

Making mess

Art is a messy business! Just put down lots of newspaper, relax, and create. It's worth it!

Encouragement

Encouragement is great for building confidence and creativity: one hundred percent encouragement equals one hundred percent creativity!

Positive attitude

We're positive! In my art classes we never say we can't do something because we simply can!

Making choices

Children's concentration is greatest when they choose the things they want to make. They make their own decisions from the start and they see them through.

Displaying

Displaying as well as talking about children's art shows it's important. Go on, put it up on the wall!

We've had lots of fun. Goodbye!